E♭ **Alto Saxophone**

Easy Great Carols

Instrumental Solos for the Intermediate Soloist

T0081912

Contents

CURNOW MUSIC

EXCLUSIVELY DISTRIBUTED BY

HAL•LEONARD® CORPORATION

7777 W. BLUEMOUND RD. P.O. BOX 13819 MILWAUKEE, WI 53213

Selected by James Curnow

Easy Great Carols
E♭ Alto Saxophone

Arranged by:
Stephen Bulla
Douglas Court
James Curnow
Paul Curnow
Timothy Johnson

Order number: CMP 0922-04-400
ISBN 90-431-2026-X
CD number: 19.052-3 CMP

Easy Great Carols

INTRODUCTION

These carols, collected from around the world, include both sacred and whimsical selections. The arrangements have been created by some of the foremost writers of instrumental music, who are internationally known for their musical compositions and arrangements. The goal of these arrangements is to allow the instrumentalist the opportunity to give praise and adoration to God through their musical abilities.

There is a separate piano accompaniment book available. This accompaniment book will work with all of the soloist books. When an accompanist is not available, the accompaniment CD (included) can be used for performance. This CD will also allow the soloist to rehearse on their own when an accompanist is not available.

The accompaniment CD contains tuning notes at the beginning to allow the soloist to adjust their intonation to the intonation of the compact disc accompaniment. Each arrangement in this collection includes a sample performance with soloist as well as a track with just the accompaniment.

May you enjoy using this collection and find it useful in extending your musical ministry.

Kindest regards,

James Curnow
President
Curnow Music Press

1. HARK! THE HERALD ANGELS SING

Track: 3 13

Arr. **James Curnow** (ASCAP)

2. SILENT NIGHT

Arr. **Paul Curnow** (ASCAP)

3. WE THREE KINGS

Arr. **Timothy Johnson** (ASCAP)

4. GOD REST YE MERRY, GENTLEMEN

Arr. **Stephen Bulla** (ASCAP)

5. JOLLY OLD ST. NICHOLAS

Arr. **Douglas Court** (ASCAP)

6. PAT-A-PAN

Arr. **Stephen Bulla** (ASCAP)

7. AWAY IN A MANGER

Track: 9 19

Arr. **James Curnow** (ASCAP)

8. UP ON THE HOUSETOP

Theme and Mini Variations

Arr. **Paul Curnow** (ASCAP)

9. WE WISH YOU A MERRY CHRISTMAS

Arr. **Douglas Court** (ASCAP)

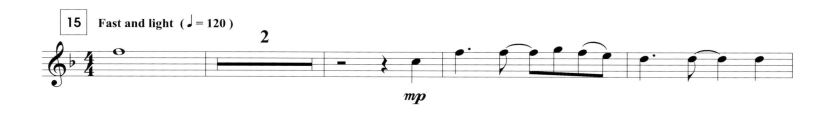

10. COVENTRY CAROL

Track: 12 22

Arr. **Timothy Johnson** (ASCAP)

TONS OF TUNES for Church

Grade 0.5-1

• arranged by Mike Hannickel and Amy Adam

A collection of 32 'fun to play' melodies arranged in easy keys for beginner instrumentalists. All the Tons of Tunes for Church books can be used together to form an ensemble. Chord symbols are included in the Piano Accompaniment book for keyboard or guitar. Titles include, Abide With Me, Now thank We All Our God, Swing Low Sweet Chariot, Onward Christian Soldiers and many more. A separate piano accompaniment book is available for concert performances.

Order number: 0871-03-400 CMP

0869-03-401 CMP Piano Accompaniment

TONS OF TUNES for the Beginner

Grade 0.5-1

• arranged by Mike Hannickel and Amy Adam

Fun and familiar tunes that beginners love to play!
There are two things that beginners really want to do: 1) play songs they RECOGNIZE and 2) play the TUNE. In TONS OF TUNES for the BEGINNER many of the easiest of familiar songs are gathered together so that young musicians can do just that - play the tunes to familiar music! Most of the songs can be performed by players who have learned only a few notes. Play along with the CD accompaniment or with any combination of solo instruments for tons of practice fun!

Order number: 0666-02-400 CMP

0672-02-401 CMP Piano Accompaniment

TONS OF TUNES for the Holidays

Grade 0.5-1

• arranged by Mike Hannickel and Amy Adam

This collection of the easiest holiday melodies allows your beginning students to have fun playing their favorite seasonal music! Any combination of solo instruments can play together. Organized by order of difficulty, these familiar songs and the included accompaniment CD are sure to motivate your students. Practice and perform with the CD accompaniment or buy the separately available piano part. Your students will want to use TONS OF TUNES for the HOLIDAYS year after year!

Order number: 0693-02-400 CMP

0699-02-401 CMP Piano Accompaniment